Comptroller of the Currency
Administrator of National Banks

Cash Accounts

Comptroller's Handbook
(Section 201)

Narrative - March 1990, Procedures - March 1998

Assets

Cash Accounts (Section 201)   Table of Contents

Cash accounts include U.S. and foreign coin and currency on hand and in transit, clearings, and cash items.

Cash

Every bank must maintain a certain amount of U.S. and foreign currency on hand. To avoid having excess nonearning assets and to minimize exposure to misappropriation and robbery, each bank should establish a policy to maintain cash balances at the minimum levels necessary to serve its customers. The amount will vary from bank to bank depending on anticipated needs of customers, with a reasonable allowance made for unusual demands.

The rates at which a bank's international division buys or sells foreign currency will not exactly match exchange rates quoted for volume book transactions or bank transfers because of such expenses as shipping charges, insurance, allocated teller salaries, and fixture cost.

Some banks do not include foreign currency in their net position reports or their monthly revaluations because of differing exchange rates and generally nominal amounts. However, the coin and currency of other countries are foreign currency assets as are loans or nostro accounts and should be included.

Clearings

Clearings are checks, drafts, notes, and other items that a bank has cashed or received for deposit that are drawn on other local banks and are cleared directly with them. Such items usually can be exchanged more efficiently among local banks, than through correspondent banks or the Federal Reserve System. Many communities with two or more banks have formally organized clearinghouse associations that have adopted rules governing members in the exchange of checks. Such associations often extend those arrangements to other nearby cities and towns.

In most banks, clearings will be found in the department responsible for processing checks. Proof and transit were once two separate functions in a bank: the proving of work (proof) and the sending of out-of-town cash items (transit) for collection. In recent years, many banks have combined those two functions. Those functions may be performed by any combination of tellers or proof clerks, by a separate proof and transit department, by a check processing department, by an outclearing department, or by some other department peculiar to the particular area of the country. The functions may be centralized or decentralized, manual or automated, depending on the size of the bank and the volume of transactions. In some large city banks, the volume of clearings is so great that the bank's proof operations are conducted on a 24-hour basis. In such cases, daily clearings customarily are determined as of a specific cutoff time. Checks processed to that time are carried in one day's totals, and checks processed after that time are carried in the following day's totals. However, no matter who performs the function or how large the bank, the objectives of a proof and transit system are the same:

- To forward items for collection so that funds are available as soon as possible.
- To distribute all incoming checks and deposits to their destinations.
- To establish whether deposit totals balance with the totals shown on deposit tickets.
- To prove the totals of general ledger entries and other transactions.
- To collect data for computing the individual customer's service charges and determining the availability of customer's funds.
- To accomplish the assigned functions at the lowest possible cost.

Cash Items

Cash items are checks or other items in the process of collection that are payable in cash upon presentation. A separate control of all such items usually is maintained on the bank's general ledger, and international division general ledger, if applicable, and is supported by a subsidiary record of individual amounts and other pertinent data. Cash items and the related records usually are in the custody of one employee at each banking office who is designated as the city cash collection, or exchange, teller.

In addition to those items carried in the separate account entitled "cash items," on the general ledger, most banks will have several sources of internal float in which irregular cash items can be concealed. Such items include any memoranda slips; checks drawn on the bank; checks returned by other banks; checks of directors, officers, employees and their interests; checks of affiliates; debits purporting to represent currency or coin shipments; notes, usually past-due; and all aged and unusual items of any nature that might involve fictitious entries, manipulations, or uncollectable accounts.

In their normal daily operations, all banks have an internal float of assets charged, on the general ledger, to the total debit to demand deposits but which cannot be charged to individual accounts because of insufficient funds, no accounts, etc. Such items are commonly known as bookkeepers' return items or rejected or unposted debits and may consist of checks received in the ordinary course of business, loan payment debits, and other debit memos. In some banks, such items are separated by the bookkeepers and an entry is made reclassifying them to a separate asset account entitled "bookkeepers' return items." Other banks do not use a separate asset account, instead the bookkeepers include the items in a subsidiary control account in the individual demand deposit ledgers. In that case, the account would have a debit balance and would be credited when the bank returns the checks to their source.

Since bookkeepers' return items usually can be returned to their source on the next business day, the balance of the bookkeepers' return item account should represent the total of only one day's returned items.

When data processing systems are in use, it is a common practice to post all properly encoded debit items, regardless of whether an overdraft is created. The resulting preliminary overdraft list, together with the items charged, then is reviewed by bank employees, and unapproved items are reversed and separated as bookkeepers' return items. The total of the resulting final overdraft list becomes the final overdraft figure shown on the general ledger. The examination of overdrafts is discussed in the "Deposit Accounts" section. The examination of international overdrafts is discussed in the "Due From Banks: Domestic and International," "Borrowed Funds: Domestic and International" and "Foreign Exchange" sections.

If the cash items are not in the process of collection, they should be included on the bank's books in an appropriate account and shown under "other assets." These are items which are payable upon presentation but which the bank has elected to accumulate for forwarding to the payor on a periodic basis, such as Series E Bonds. If the items are not immediately payable in cash upon presentation, or if they were not paid when presented and, after a predetermined period of time, require further collection effort, they also should be included in a non-cash asset account, such as "suspense resources," and shown under "other assets." Examples are checks held to avoid overdrafts and other checks for which there are no funds for immediate payment. Many banks set a 3-day limit, after which all items not collected must automatically be transferred from "cash items" to "suspense resources."

Currency Transactions

The Financial Recordkeeping and Reporting regulations, 31 CFR 103, require financial institutions to maintain records that might be useful in criminal, tax, or regulatory investigations. They also seek to identify persons who attempt to avoid payment of taxes through transfers of cash to or from foreign accounts. Amendments to the regulations are expected to facilitate the investigations of narcotics trafficking, tax evasion, and other criminal activities. 12 CFR 11, Reports of Crimes and Suspected Crimes, establishes guidelines for banks to refer to appropriate authorities instances when known or suspected evasion of the Bank Secrecy Act reporting requirements have occurred. The examination procedures for determining compliance with the regulations require the examiner to ascertain the quality of the bank's auditing procedures and operating standards relating to 31 CFR 103 and to determine whether the bank has established a Bank Secrecy Act compliance program as required by 12 CFR 21.21. Examiners also determine the adequacy of written policies and bank training programs. Detailed guidelines for assessing the effectiveness of Bank Secrecy Act compliance are included in the Comptroller's Handbook for Compliance.

Cash Accounts (Section 201)   Examination Procedures

General Procedures

Objective: Determine the scope of the examination of cash accounts.

1. Review the following documents to identify any previous problems that require follow up:

    ☐ Supervisory strategy in the OCC's electronic information system.
    ☐ EIC's scope memorandum.
    ☐ Previous ROE and overall summary comments.
    ☐ Working papers from the previous examination.
    ☐ Audit reports, and working papers, if necessary.
    ☐ Correspondence memorandum.

2. From the EIC, obtain the results of his/her analysis of the UBPR, BERT, and other applicable OCC reports. Identify any concerns, trends, or changes in cash accounts.

3. Obtain and review those reports used to supervise cash accounts, including:

    ☐ Balance sheet and general ledger.
    ☐ Cash item listings.
    ☐ Nonledger item listings.
    ☐ Foreign currency revaluations.

4. Determine, during early discussions with management:

    • How management supervises the cash accounts.
    • Any significant changes in policies, procedures, personnel, or controls relating to cash accounts since the last examination.
    • Any internal or external factors that could affect cash accounts.

5. Based on the performance of these steps and discussions with the bank EIC, determine the scope of this examination and its objectives.

Note: Select steps necessary to meet objectives from among the following examination procedures. All steps are seldom required in an examination.

Quantity of Risk

Conclusion: The quantity of risk is (low, moderate, high).

Objective: Determine the level of cash account exposure and identify any undue compliance, transaction, foreign currency translation, or price risk in the general ledger cash accounts.

1.   Review OCC and internal bank reports and evaluate the level of:

   • Compliance risk arising from violations of, or noncompliance with, laws and regulations.
   • Price risk or foreign currency translation risk arising from inaccuracies or deficiencies in the foreign currency revaluations.
   • Transaction risk arising from inadequate controls.

2.   If the bank has significant exposure in cash accounts due to compliance, foreign currency translation, or transaction risks, evaluate the steps management has taken to address those risks.

3.   Scan the general ledger cash accounts for any unusual items or abnormal fluctuations.

4.   Obtain teller settlement recap sheets or similar documents as of the examination date and do the following:

   • Agree the totals to the general ledger.
   • Scan for reasonableness.
   • Evaluate conformity to bank policy.

5.   Review detailed listings of all cash items, including any bank items which are carried in the general ledger under "Other Assets," and any items held in teller drawers or not otherwise recorded on the bank's general ledger, and do the following:

   • Agree listings to general ledger balances.
   • Scan for propriety.
   • Determine compliance with bank policy.
   • Evaluate reasons why any cash items are not recorded on the bank's

---

books.

6. Review tellers' over and short accounts for recurring patterns and any large or unusual items and follow up as necessary by:

   - Investigating differences centered in any one teller.
   - Determining whether corrective action has been taken, if necessary.

7. Determine, through discussions with responsible bank officials and a review of documentation, whether any defalcations and/or mysterious disappearances of cash since the preceding examination have been properly reported pursuant to 12 CFR 21.11.

8. Review foreign currency control ledgers and dollar book value equivalents. Consider:

   - Accuracy of calculations and booking procedures.
   - Unusual fluctuations.
   - Concentrations.
   - Unusual items.

9. Review international division revaluation calculations and procedures if performed by the cash account operations staff. (The bank's accounting/auditing department may revalue cash accounts together with other foreign currency ledger and future exchange accounts).

10. Discuss any concerns or significant risks with management.

Quality of Risk Management

Conclusion: The quality of risk management is (strong, satisfactory, weak).

Policy

Conclusion: The board (has/has not) established effective policies governing cash accounts.

Objective: Determine if policies regarding cash accounts are adequate.

1. Does the bank have policies addressing major risk areas? Examples include:

   - A policy requiring that all cash items uncollected for a period of 30 days be charged off.
   - A policy against allowing teller "kitties."

2. Review the bank's policies regarding cash accounts. Consider:

   - Are written policies adequately reviewed and approved?
   - Do written policies/procedures adequately address the bank's potential risks from cash accounts?
   - Do policies comply with appropriate laws and regulations?

Processes

Conclusion: Management and the board (have/have not) established effective processes relative to cash accounts.

Objective: Determine if processes regarding cash accounts are adequate and in compliance with laws and regulations.

1. Review the bank's processes relative to daily activities involving cash account transactions. Consider:

   - Did the most recent compliance examination uncover any weaknesses or violations of law or regulations dealing with the Bank Secrecy Act

---

(BSA)?   If violations were noted:
- – Determine whether corrective action has been taken.
- – Test subsequent compliance with any law or regulation so noted.
- In the absence of a recent compliance examination, determine whether there is any reason to believe that BSA compliance should be tested at this time. If so, refer to the detailed guidelines in the "Bank Secrecy Act" Booklet (CCE-BSA).
- Did the bank's most recent current compliance audit uncover any weaknesses or violations of law and regulation dealing with the BSA?

2.   Determine whether adequate internal controls, policies, practices, and procedures have been implemented for cash accounts in the following areas:

Cash on Hand

- Tellers, including relief tellers, have sole access to their own cash supply and all spare keys are kept under dual control.
- Tellers have their own vault cubicle or controlled cash drawer in which to store their cash supply.
- When a teller is leaving for vacation or for any other extended period of time, that teller's cash supply is counted.
- Each teller's cash is verified periodically on a surprise basis by an officer or other designated official. (If so, is a record of such account retained)?
- Cash drawers or teller cages are provided with locking devices to protect the cash during periods of teller absences.
- A specified limit is in effect for each teller's cash.
- Each teller's cash is checked daily to an independent control from the proof or accounting control department.
- Tellers differences are cleared daily.
- An individual cumulative over and short record is maintained for all persons handling cash and the record is reviewed by management.
- Each teller prepares and signs a daily proof sheet detailing currency, coin, and cash items.
- Large teller differences are required to be reported to a responsible official for clearance.
- Teller transactions are identified through use of a teller stamp.

- Teller transfers made by tickets or blotter entries are verified by both tellers.
- Maximum amounts are established for tellers cashing checks or allowing withdrawal from time deposit accounts without officer approval.
- The currency at each location includes a supply of bait money.
- Tellers are provided with operational guidelines on check cashing procedures and dollar limits.
- A specific limit is in effect for reserve cash and a record is maintained showing amounts and denominations.
- Reserve cash is under dual custody.
- If the bank uses teller machines:
    - The master key is controlled by someone independent of the teller function.
    - The daily proof is performed by someone other than a teller.
    - Keys are removed by the teller during any absence.
    - Dual control is maintained over mail deposits.
- The night depository box is under dual lock system.
- The withdrawal of night deposits is made under dual control.
- Regarding night depository transactions:
    - Written contracts are in effect.
    - Customers are provided with locking bags.
    - The following procedures are completed under dual control:
        - Opening of bags.
        - Initial recording of bag numbers, envelope numbers, and deposit names in the register.
        - Counting and verification of the contents.
- Regarding vault control:
    - A register is maintained which is signed by the individuals opening and closing the vault.
    - Time clock settings are checked by a second officer.
    - The vault is under dual control.
    - Combinations are changed periodically and every time there is a change in custodianship.
- Tellers are prohibited from processing their own checks.
- Tellers are required to clear all checks from their funds daily.
- Tellers are prevented from having access to accounting department records.
- Teller duties are restricted to teller operations.

Cash Dispensing Machines

- Daily access to the automated teller machine (ATM) is made under dual control.
- When maintenance is being performed on a machine, with or without cash in it, a representative of the bank is required to be in attendance.
- Combinations and keys to the machines are controlled (if so, indicate controls).
- The machines and the related system have built-in controls that:
  - Limit the amount of cash and the number of times dispensed during a specified period (if so, indicate detail).
  - Capture the card if the wrong PIN (Personal Identification Number) is consecutively used.
- The machine automatically shuts down after it experiences recurring errors.
- Lighting around the machine is provided.
- The machine captures cards of other banks or invalid cards.
- If the machine is operated "off-line," it has negative file capabilities for present and future needs that include lists of lost, stolen, or other undesirable cards that should be captured.
- Usage of an ATM by an individual customer in excess of that customer's past history is indicated on a "suspicious activity" report to be checked out by bank management (e.g., three uses during the past three days as compared to a history of one use per month).
- Safeguards have been implemented at the ATM to prevent disclosure of a customer's PIN during use by others observing the PIN pad.
- "Fish-proof" receptacles are provided for customers to dispose of printed receipts, rather than insecure trash cans, etc.
- A communication interruption between an ATM and the central processing unit triggers an alarm system.
- Alarm devices are connected to all automated teller machines.
- For on-line operations, all messages to and from the central processing unit and the ATM are protected from tapping, message insertion, modification of message, or surveillance by message encryption (scrambling technique). (One recognized encryption formula is the National Bureau of Standards Algorithm).
- PIN's are mailed separately from cards.

- Bank personnel who have custody of cards are prohibited from also having custody of PIN's at any stage (issuance, verification, or reissuance).
- Magnetic stripe cards are encrypted (scrambled) using an adequate algorithm (formula) including a total message control.
- Encryption keys, (i.e., scramble plugs) are under dual control of personnel not associated with operations or card issuance.
- Captured cards are under dual control or persons not associated with bank operation card issuance or PIN issuance.
- Blank plastic and magnetic stripe readers are under dual control.
- All cards are issued with set expiration dates.
- Transaction journals are provided that enable management to determine every transaction or attempted transaction at the ATM.

Cash Items

- Returned items are handled by someone other than the teller who originated the transaction.
- An officer reviews the disposition of all cash items over a specified dollar limit.
- A daily report made of all cash items is reviewed and initiated by the bank's operations officer or other designated official.
- The bank's present procedures forbid the holding of overdraft checks in the cash item account.
- All cash items are reviewed at least monthly by the board of directors or an appropriate designee.
- Cash items recommended for charge off, are reviewed and approved by the board of directors, a designated committee thereof, or an officer with no operational responsibilities.

Proof and Transit

- Individuals working in the proof and transit department are precluded from working in other departments of the bank.
- The handling of cash letters is such that:
  - They are prepared and sent on a daily basis.
  - They are photographed before they leave the bank.
  - A copy of proof or hand-run tape is properly identified and returned.

- Records of cash letters sent to correspondent banks are maintained with identification of the subject bank, date, and amount.
  - Remittances for cash letters are received by employees independent of those who send out the cash letters.
- All entries to the general ledger are either originated or proved by the proof department.
- All entries prepared by the general ledger and/or customer accounts department are reviewed by responsible supervisory personnel other than the person preparing the entry.
- Errors detected by the proof operator in proving deposits are corrected by another employee or designated officer.
- All postings to the general ledger and subsidiary ledgers are supported by source documents.
- Returned items are:
  - Handled by an independent section of the department or delivered unopened to personnel not responsible for preparing cash letters.
  - Reviewed periodically by responsible supervisory personnel to determine that items are being handled correctly and are clearing on a timely basis.
  - Scrutinized for employee items.
  - Reviewed for large or repeat items.
- Holdover items are:
  - Appropriately identified in the general ledger.
  - Handled by an independent section of the department.
  - Reviewed periodically by responsible supervisory personnel to determine that items are clearing on a timely basis.
- The proof and transit department maintain a procedures manual describing the key operating procedures and functions within the department.
- Items reported missing from cash letters are promptly traced and a copy sent for credit.
- There is a formal system to insure that work distributed to proof machine operators is formally rotated.
- Proof machine operators are prohibited from:
  - Filing checks or deposit slips.
  - Preparing deposit account statements.
- Proof machine operators are instructed to report unusually large deposits or withdrawals to a responsible officer.

International Division

- Foreign currency control ledgers and dollar book value equivalents are posted accurately.
- Each foreign currency is revalued at least monthly and profit and loss entries are passed to the appropriate income accounts.
- Revaluation calculations, including the rates periodically used, are reviewed for accuracy by someone other than the foreign currency tellers.
- The internal auditor periodically reviews for accuracy revaluation calculations, including the verification of rates used and the resulting general ledger entries.

3.   Determine whether bank security guidelines have been established that provide detailed information on the development and maintenance of a security program (see 12 CFR 21—Subpart A and Security Checklist). Consider:

- Location and physical specifications.
- Crimes against the office.
- Use of armed guards.
- Local law enforcement.
- Alarm systems.
- Vaults and safes.
- Surveillance systems.
- Cash control.

4.   If violations were noted in any cash account activities or processes, determine whether corrective action was taken.

Personnel

Conclusion: Bank officers and employees (are/are not) operating in conformance with the established guidelines.

Objective: Given the size and complexity of the bank, determine if bank management/personnel possesses and displays acceptable knowledge and technical skills in managing and performing the duties related to cash accounts.

1.   Assess bank management's and/or significant personnel's knowledge and technical skills related to cash management based on conclusions developed while performing these procedures.

2.   Determine if bank officers and employees are operating in compliance with bank policies and procedures.

Controls

Conclusion: Management (has/has not) established effective control systems.

Objective: Assess the quality of control systems.

1.   Determine the effectiveness of the audit function in identifying risk in cash accounts and foreign currency transactions (if applicable). Consider the following:

   - Scope and coverage of review(s).
   - Frequency of review(s).
   - Qualifications of audit personnel.
   - Comprehensiveness and accuracy of findings/recommendations.
   - Adequacy and timeliness of follow up.

2.   Evaluate the effectiveness of the compliance program in identifying compliance risk in cash accounts and foreign currency transactions (if applicable). Consider the following:

   - Scope and coverage. Does the review test for compliance with the applicable laws, rulings, and regulations?
   - If violations/exceptions were noted, determine if the bank took appropriate corrective action.
   - Adequacy and timeliness of follow up.

3.   Determine the effectiveness of any other control systems used by management and the board in the risk management of cash accounts and foreign currency transactions (if applicable).

Conclusion

Objective: Determine overall conclusions and convey findings regarding cash account activities.

1.   Identify any cash accounts receiving inadequate supervision. Discuss them with the bank EIC.

2.   Prepare written conclusion comments to communicate findings to the EIC. Consider:

   - Internal control exceptions.
   - Deficiencies or noncompliance with written policies and procedures.
   - Uncorrected audit deficiencies.
   - Violations of laws and regulations.
   - Inaccurate booking of U.S. dollar book value equivalents for foreign currencies.
   - Inaccurate revaluation calculations and procedures performed by cash account operations staff.
   - Any concerns and/or recommendations.

3.   Determine the impact on the aggregate and direction of risk assessments for any applicable risks identified by performing the above procedures. Examiners should refer to guidance provided under the OCC's large and community bank risk assessment programs.

   - Risk Categories: Compliance, Credit, Foreign Currency Translation, Interest Rate, Liquidity, Price, Reputation, Strategic, Transaction
   - Risk Conclusions: High, Moderate, or Low
   - Risk Direction: Increasing, Stable, or Decreasing

4.   Determine in consultation with the EIC, if the risks identified are significant enough to merit bringing them to the board's attention in the report of examination. If so, prepare items for inclusion under the headings Matters Requiring Board Attention.

   - MRBA should cover practices that:
     - Deviate from sound fundamental principles and are likely to result

in financial deterioration if not addressed
   – Result in substantive noncompliance with laws.
 • MRBA should discuss:
   – Causative factors contributing to the problem
   – Consequences of inaction
   – Management's commitment for corrective action
   – The time frame and person(s) responsible for corrective action.

5. As appropriate, discuss with bank officer(s) the following:

 • The quantity of risk assumed by the bank from cash account exposures. Include an assessment of the impact of the cash account exposure on the nine risk areas.
 • The quality of the bank's process to manage risk created in cash account exposures.
 • The adequacy of policies and procedures.
 • The manner in which bank officers operate in conformance with established policies.
 • The adequacy of information on cash accounts available for management and the board of directors.

6. As appropriate, prepare a brief cash accounts comment for inclusion in the report of examination. Consider:

 • Adequacy of policies, processes, personnel, and control systems.
 • Any deficiencies reviewed with management and any remedial actions recommended.

7. Prepare a memorandum or update the work program with any information that will facilitate future examinations.

8. Update the OCC's electronic information system and any applicable report of examination schedules or tables.

9. Organize and reference working papers in accordance with OCC guidance.

The Bank Security Manual published by the Bank Administration Institute is a comprehensive guide to bank security and provides detailed information on the development and maintenance of a security program. The following questionnaire relating to security programs for banks was obtained from that manual.

Location and Physical Specifications

1. Are all windows clear of obstruction, permitting a clear view of the interior?

2. Are protection equipment and FBI investigation signs prominently displayed on doors?

3. Have exterior lights been installed to illuminate all darkened or shadowed areas around the bank?

4. Are the bank lighting systems, interior and exterior, maintained in good condition?

5. Is there traffic near the bank during the night?

6. Are neighborhood residents and police officials instructed to contact a bank officer if the lighting fails?

7. Is the vault area illuminated at night?

8. Does the bank have an emergency lighting source?

9. Are the locks on exterior doors and windows tamper-resistant?

10. Are all entrances and exits to the bank building placed for greatest security?

11. Are doors and windows that are not readily visible from the street equipped with steel bars or other burglar-resistant materials?

12. Are door and window hinge pins securely fastened so that they cannot be broken or forced?

13. Are all unusual entrances, such as exhaust fans, ventilators, air conditioner intakes, skylights, sidewalk manholes, etc., protected by an alarm system, steel bars or other protective materials?

14. Are entrances from the basement or upper floors secured by locks or an alarm system?

15. Is there a regular procedure for securing side and back doors while the bank is open for business?

16. Is there only one entrance to the public lobby?

17. Does the layout give bank personnel standing anywhere in the lobby a wide-angle view of teller stations and other vulnerable areas?

18. Does the design of lobby teller stations reduce exposure?

19. Are all entrances to the teller work area locked while the bank is open and/or while customers are in the bank?

20. Are walk-up or drive-in teller stations constructed of bullet-resistant materials?

21. Are the special security requirements for separate teller stations recognized?

Crimes against the Office

1. Has the office been free of robberies and attempted robberies for the past 5 years?

2. Has the office been free of burglaries and attempted burglaries for the past 5 years?

3. Has the office been free of non-employee larcenies and attempted larcenies for the past 5 years?

4.   If crimes have occurred, have steps been taken to prevent their recurrence?

Use of Armed Guards

1.   Are armed guards on duty in the lobby during banking hours?

2.   Are the guards trained to use firearms?

3.   Are guards instructed what to do in a holdup?

4.   Are guards stationed in locations that provide a maximum view of the banking lobby without having their backs to the door?

5.   Are guards utilized strictly as guards and not to perform other duties in and outside the bank?

6.   Are guards instructed to approach suspicious persons and offer assistance?

7.   Does the bank use armed guards in the office during non-banking hours?

8.   Is the guard program or schedule varied from time to time?

Local Law Enforcement

1.   Is the banking office located within regularly patrolled areas?

2.   Is the anticipated time lag for the arrival of law enforcement officers less than 5 minutes after a summons?

3.   Do police officials periodically check the bank during non-business hours?

4.   Have policemen been encouraged to be in the vicinity of the bank at opening and closing time?

5.   Since enactment of the Bank Protection Act, have local law enforcement representatives been invited to inspect the bank's premises and review its

security program?

6. Are regularly scheduled meetings held with local law enforcement representatives?

Alarm Systems

1. Are there alarm activating devices at lobby teller stations?

2. Are existing alarm systems wireless?

3. Are there alarm activating devices at drive-in and walk-in teller stations?

4. Can activating devices be operated unobtrusively?

5. Are alarm activators installed in the vault, restrooms, or other areas where employees might be held?

6. Do the alarm systems indicate circuit failure, malfunctions or tampering instantly?

7. Is the alarm system tested periodically?

8. Is there an emergency power supply for use if the regular supply fails?

9. Are reporting locations for alarms at a central station or a local law enforcement office in service 24 hours per day?

10. Does the bank have intrusion alarms?

11. Does the burglar alarm system activate a loud bell that is audible both inside and outside the premises?

Vaults and Safes

1. Are vaults made of steel-reinforced concrete at least 12 inches thick, and vault doors of drill- and torch-resistant material at least 3 1/2 inches thick?

2. Are vaults equipped with a dial combination lock, a time lock, and a substantial, lockable "day gate"?

3. Do safes weigh at least 750 pounds when empty, or are they securely anchored to the premises?

4. Are safe doors equipped with a combination lock and a relocking device that will effectively lock them if the combination lock is punched?

5. Do night depositories have receptacle chests with cast or welded steel walls at least 1 inch thick on all sides?

6. Are night depositories equipped with burglar alarms, and are they designed to prevent the "fishing" and "trapping" of deposits?

7. Are the vault walls, floor, ceiling, and door protected by an alarm system?

8. Are safe deposit boxes maintained in the cash vault or another vault providing at least equal protection?

9. Is the vault equipped with an emergency air ventilation system?

10. Is the vault equipped with an alarm or telephone so that an employee locked in the vault can sound an alert?

Surveillance Systems

1. Does the bank have surveillance cameras?

2. Is the operation of the cameras automatic and continuous?

3. Do the cameras cover all exits and tellers' positions?

4. Are the cameras used to take pictures of persons cashing checks and for other identification purposes?

Cash Control

1. Is opening the vault under dual control?

2. Is the vault opened at the latest practical time before the bank's opening for business?

3. Is the vault closed as soon as practical after the bank's closing hour?

4. Is the currency in each banking office kept at a minimum?

5. Is reserve currency protected by being placed in either a delayed time lock chest or a vault not accessible from the lobby?

6. Is a supply of bait money included in the vault cash?

7. Is there a standard operating procedure for the safe shipment of currency not needed at each office?

8. Is the currency at each teller's station kept at a minimum?

9. Are tellers instructed to keep cash out of the customer's reach?

10. Is there a standard operating procedure for the quick and safe removal of excess currency and other valuables from exposed areas?

11. Are tellers instructed to take appropriate measures to safeguard valuables whenever it is necessary to leave their stations?

12. Does the currency at each teller's station include bait money?

13. Is the bait money packaged and stored so that it will be given out in the event of a robbery?

14. Are all supplies of currency, negotiable securities, and similar valuables stored during non-business hours in vaults or safes that provide burglary protection?

15. Are precautions taken to prevent theft of all unissued forms, checks, money orders, and so forth?

16. Is access to the reserve cash supply protected by dual control or joint

custody procedures?

17. Are tellers and other lobby personnel regularly trained in robbery and post-robbery procedures?

18. Is there a documented procedure for opening and closing the building and vaults that protects against attack?

19. Are procedures established for the maintenance and testing of all security devices?

www.ingramcontent.com/pod-product-compliance
Lightning Source LLC
Chambersburg PA
CBHW080757290526
45790CB00008B/3490